Countering Sexual Violence in Conflict

COUNCIL *on*
FOREIGN
RELATIONS

Center for Preventive Action
Women and Foreign Policy

DISCUSSION PAPER

Countering Sexual Violence in Conflict

Jamille Bigio
Rachel Vogelstein

September 2017

The Council on Foreign Relations (CFR) is an independent, nonpartisan membership organization, think tank, and publisher dedicated to being a resource for its members, government officials, business executives, journalists, educators and students, civic and religious leaders, and other interested citizens in order to help them better understand the world and the foreign policy choices facing the United States and other countries. Founded in 1921, CFR carries out its mission by maintaining a diverse membership, with special programs to promote interest and develop expertise in the next generation of foreign policy leaders; convening meetings at its headquarters in New York and in Washington, DC, and other cities where senior government officials, members of Congress, global leaders, and prominent thinkers come together with CFR members to discuss and debate major international issues; supporting a Studies Program that fosters independent research, enabling CFR scholars to produce articles, reports, and books and hold roundtables that analyze foreign policy issues and make concrete policy recommendations; publishing *Foreign Affairs*, the preeminent journal on international affairs and U.S. foreign policy; sponsoring Independent Task Forces that produce reports with both findings and policy prescriptions on the most important foreign policy topics; and providing up-to-date information and analysis about world events and American foreign policy on its website, CFR.org.

The Council on Foreign Relations takes no institutional positions on policy issues and has no affiliation with the U.S. government. All views expressed in its publications and on its website are the sole responsibility of the author or authors.

For further information about CFR or this paper, please write to the Council on Foreign Relations, 58 East 68th Street, New York, NY 10065, or call Communications at 212.434.9888. Visit CFR's website, www.cfr.org.

This report is printed on paper that is FSC® Chain-of-Custody Certified by a printer who is certified by BM TRADA North America Inc.

Contents

Acknowledgments

This report was produced under the guidance of CFR's advisory committee on sexual violence in conflict, a distinguished group of experts from the government, multilateral organizations, academia, and the private and public sectors. Over the past several months, members of this advisory committee have participated in meetings, reviewed drafts, and shared research and insights from their work. The report has been enhanced considerably by the expertise of this advisory group, and we are thankful for members' participation. The views expressed here and any errors are our own.

A special acknowledgment is extended to James M. Lindsay, CFR's director of studies, for his support for this project, and Paul Stares, senior fellow for conflict prevention and director of the Center for Preventive Action, for his partnership in this effort. We are grateful to Patricia Dorff, Liz Dana, Julie Hersh, Sarah Collman, and Helia Ighani for their review of previous drafts, and to Anne Connell and Alyssa Dougherty for their excellent assistance in the production of this paper. U.S. officials also provided feedback that significantly contributed to the report.

This report was written under the auspices of the Women and Foreign Policy program, whose work on women, peace, and security is supported by the Compton Foundation. The report was written in collaboration with the Center for Preventive Action and made possible by the generous support of the Carnegie Corporation of New York.

Jamille Bigio
Rachel Vogelstein

Introduction

The victims of today's armed conflicts are more likely to be civilians than soldiers. Armies and armed groups often subject noncombatants—particularly women and children—to conflict-related sexual violence, such as rape, sexual slavery, and forced marriage. Despite international recognition of this devastating abuse as a crime against humanity, sexual violence continues to plague conflicts from the Democratic Republic of Congo (DRC) to Syria. This practice has also proliferated among extremist groups, including Boko Haram in Nigeria and the self-proclaimed Islamic State in Iraq and Syria. Additionally, sexual violence has tarnished the operations of peacekeepers charged with protecting civilians, thereby undermining the integrity and effectiveness of international peacekeeping institutions across the globe.

Sexual violence in conflict is not simply a gross violation of human rights—it is also a security challenge. Such violence has consequences that increase the costs of armed conflict, rendering its management more difficult. Wartime rape fuels displacement, weakens governance, and destabilizes communities, thereby inhibiting postconflict reconciliation and imperiling long-term stability. When committed by troops, it can represent a lack of discipline associated with weak command and control, which makes military units less effective in advancing their mission. Yet current security-sector efforts to address sexual violence in conflict are inadequate, plagued by insufficient training for peacekeepers, limited accountability through national and international judicial systems, and resource gaps.

Combating conflict-related sexual violence merits a higher place on the U.S. foreign policy agenda. Although the U.S. government has taken modest steps to address sexual violence in conflict under successive Republican and Democratic administrations, more action is needed. To counter such violence, the Donald J. Trump administration should require training on conflict-related sexual violence in U.S.

security cooperation efforts; expand the number of women serving in militaries, police, and peacekeeping forces around the world; increase accountability for the crime of sexual violence; and undermine terrorist financing streams raised through the abduction of women and children. These steps will help the United States and its allies respond effectively to the security threat posed by conflict-related sexual violence and advance U.S. interests in peace and stability.

Understanding Sexual Violence in Conflict

Sexual violence in conflict is not a new phenomenon. Throughout history, armies have considered rape to be one of the legitimate spoils of war, and sexual violence was tacitly accepted as unavoidable through the early twentieth century. In recent decades, however, successive legal rulings have outlawed sexual violence and recognized it as a crime against humanity and war crime, beginning in 1992, when the UN Security Council declared the massive, organized, and systematic detention and rape of women in the former Yugoslavia to be an international crime. This decision paved the way for more robust adjudication of such incidents worldwide. Today, sexual violence in conflict can violate national criminal law and international law and constitute a war crime, crime against humanity, or act of genocide—even in the absence of death (see appendix 1).[1] It can be perpetrated against women, men, girls, or boys by uniformed members of an army, members of a nonstate armed group or terrorist organization, or civilians. Perpetrators are predominantly but not exclusively male; examples from the DRC, Rwanda, and elsewhere demonstrate that women have played active roles in all aspects of armed conflict, including ordering or perpetrating rape.[2]

In 2017, the United Nations identified forty-six parties to ten conflicts as "credibly suspected" of committing rape or other forms of sexual violence; seven of the parties were designated as "terrorist groups" because of links with the Islamic State and al-Qaeda.[3] Yet though some conflicts are characterized by widespread sexual violence, not all are. A significant number of armies and rebels in recent wars did not rape civilians: one analysis of 177 armed groups in twenty African countries found that 59 percent were not reported to have committed sexual violence.[4] Another analysis of ninety-one civil wars between 1980 and 2012 revealed that 17 percent were not characterized by sexual violence.[5] Variation in prevalence is driven in part by leaders of armed organizations who, based on ideology, alternatively may order, tolerate, or prohibit rape by their soldiers; therefore, understanding the conditions that foster sexual violence in conflict is critical to improving responses to the practice in different contexts.[6] Contrary to conventional wisdom, factors such as state failure, prevalence of contraband funding, and abduction of fighting forces are better predictors of sexual violence than ethnic warring.[7]

Conflict-related sexual violence varies widely in form and severity. Groups or individuals commit conflict-related sexual violence for any number—or combination—of reasons, including as a deliberate tactic of war, an act of opportunism, a form of troop payment, an effort to build group cohesion, or a tool of ethnic destruction.

TACTIC OF WAR AND TERROR

Sexual violence in conflict zones can be employed as a deliberate tactic to terrorize civilians. The strategic nature of such violence is manifested by the selective targeting of victims from opposing ethnic, religious, or political groups, mirroring the fault lines of the broader conflict or crisis. The brutality of conflict-related sexual violence, as well as the shame and stigma suffered by survivors, is integral to the logic behind sexual violence as a tactic of war and terror. Armed or extremist groups and individual aggressors employ this tool to denigrate the enemy, create stigma, and unravel protective kinship networks.

In recent years, conflict-related sexual violence has emerged as a core element of the ideology and operation of extremist groups, such as Boko Haram and the Islamic State.[8] These groups use sexual violence to terrorize populations into compliance, displace civilians from strategic areas, and entrench an ideology of suppressing women's rights to control reproduction and provide labor.[9] Some violent extremist groups also promote the enslavement of women and girls as a form of currency in a shadow economy, generating revenue from sex trafficking, sexual slavery, and extortion through ransom. For example, the United Nations estimates that ransom payments extracted by the Islamic State from the Yazidi community amounted to between $35 million and $45 million in 2014 alone.[10] And even as the Islamic State loses territory and control of physical resources, the group continues to profit from the enslavement of an estimated two thousand women and girls, many of whom are bartered and sold as commodities.[11]

Sexual violence is also used by state forces, armed groups, and terrorists as a form of torture against captured belligerents and their relatives and civilians, both to impose punishment and as a tool to extract information.[12] Use of this practice as a torture method, primarily against men and boys but occasionally against women and girls, has been documented in a range of conflict situations, including during Peru's civil war between 1980 and 2000, against Sunni detainees in Iraqi prisons in the 2000s, and in Syria's prisons today.[13]

OPPORTUNISM BEFORE, DURING, AND AFTER CONFLICT

Sexual violence in conflict also can proliferate in the absence of a deliberate strategy, flourishing under a command structure that fosters a climate of impunity. State collapse and the dissolution of protective political, legal, economic, and social systems have been shown to contribute to sexual violence carried out by state armed groups, rebel groups, peacekeeping and security forces, and civilians in times of upheaval.[14] Among state and nonstate forces, sexual violence frequently occurs in conjunction with other opportunistic crimes against civilians, such as looting and killing.[15]

State forces are more likely than rebels or pro-government militias to be reported as perpetrators of sexual violence.[16] State forces can employ sexual violence strategically or opportunistically in detention facilities and during operations against civilians, such as in the context of urban warfare, during house searches, and at checkpoints. One study, for example, found that in African conflicts between 2000 and 2009, 64 percent of government actors were reported as perpetrators of sexual violence, compared with 31 percent of rebel groups and 29 percent of other militias.[17]

Peacekeepers and security forces tasked with protecting civilian populations also commit sexual violence against highly vulnerable people under their protection: a 2017 report found an estimated two thousand allegations of sexual exploitation and abuse by peacekeepers and UN personnel around the world.[18]

PAYMENT AND INCENTIVES

Conflict-related sexual violence sometimes manifests as a currency in which women and girls are treated as wages of war, provided implicitly or explicitly to fighters as a form of in-kind compensation for enlistment or service. For example, UN reports document that pro-government militias in South Sudan were allowed, and even told, to rape women in lieu of payment of government wages in recent years.[19]

A number of extremist groups—including Boko Haram and the Islamic State—offer sexual compensation to recruit young men through the promise of "wives" or sex slaves. The Islamic State, for example, deftly uses social media and its slickly produced online magazines, *Dabiq* and *Rumiyah*, to connect sexual violence to the spiritual fulfillment of recruits who serve a vital role in promulgating the next generation of an Islamic caliphate.[20] Online recruiters promise men beautiful brides and young women loving husbands. In practice, the Islamic State provides thousands of male recruits with kidnapped women and girls as wives and traps many female recruits in dorms for indoctrination and forced marriage.[21] Some women, however, are willingly recruited by these extremist organizations to support radical ideologies and become the wives of fighters, often in hope of gaining freedoms and access to resources.[22]

Armed groups that recruit through abduction or press-ganging are more likely to perpetrate rape: a review of ninety-one civil wars, for example, found that state and nonstate groups employing forced recruitment practices committed significantly more rape against civilians.[23] Groups that recruit members through abduction have less internal social cohesion than groups that recruit volunteers, and thus attempt to build social bonds and unit cohesion through rape, particularly gang rape, of women or men.[24]

ETHNIC DESTRUCTION

In its most extreme manifestation, mass rape is used by armed groups as part of a broader strategy of ethnic cleansing against a perceived enemy. As defined in Articles II and III of the 1948 Convention on the Prevention and Punishment of the Crime of Genocide, acts of sexual violence in conflict can constitute genocide—even absent death—when used to instill terror in a civilian population of a certain national, ethnic, racial, or religious group; force dislocation; and force pregnancy so that the aggressing actor "invades" the targeted population's bloodlines in order to destroy future generations.[25]

Campaigns of genocidal rape have been documented during conflicts in Bosnia, East Timor, Guatemala, Rwanda, and Uganda, among others.[26] During the 1994 Rwandan genocide, for example, mass rapes were an integral part of the concerted campaign by Hutu politicians and militia leaders to rid the country of its Tutsi minority. Rwandan women were subjected to sexual violence on a massive scale, perpetrated primarily by members of the infamous Hutu militia group known as the Interahamwe, as well as by civilians incited to violence by extremist propaganda and threats.[27]

In recent years, Burmese government forces reportedly have committed ethnically motivated rape and gang rape against women and girls amid escalating conflict in the Rakhine State. Rights groups assert that this sexual violence is not random or opportunistic, but is rather part of a systematic attack against the Rohingya minority. Witness accounts detail how perpetrators in many cases threatened or insulted victims during assaults using language derogatory to Rohingya Muslims.[28]

Implications for U.S. Interests

Sexual violence in armed conflict—whether committed by armies, nonstate armed groups, violent extremist groups, peacekeeping forces, or civilians—damages a nation's prospects for stability and postconflict recovery. Conflict-related sexual violence undermines command and control, increases displacement, weakens governance, imposes devastating financial costs, and complicates reconciliation, thereby imperiling global security. Rape in wartime also represents an affront to U.S. values and undermines public support for international institutions that are critical to advancing U.S. interests in stability.

IMPERILED COMMAND AND CONTROL

Sexual violence committed by troops can represent a lack of discipline associated with weak command and control or a poor focus on objectives. For example, in the DRC, a mass rape of more than 150 civilians in 2011 was attributed to lax command and control structures by local armed forces.[29] Pervasive sexual violence by state forces often indicates that a command hierarchy is simply too weak to enforce a policy forbidding this crime; indeed, recent reports from the UN special representative of the secretary-general for sexual violence in conflict specifically link spikes in sexual violence to weak command and troop discipline.[30]

In security partnerships, rape and other civilian abuses damage the mutual trust that is critical to successful collaboration. For example, the director general of the international military staff of the North Atlantic Treaty Organization (NATO) reports that conflict-related sexual violence obstructs the success of NATO priorities and slows down conflict-resolution processes.[31] Because military units and law enforcement bodies that respect human rights and prevent sexual violence are more effective at promoting security, the failure to incorporate training on sexual violence prevention into security cooperation efforts with foreign allies undermines U.S. interests.[32]

INCREASED DISPLACEMENT

Conflict-related sexual violence also displaces people from their homes, which deprives them and their families of their livelihoods, property, and access to health and educational services, thereby undermining postconflict economic and social recovery.[33] Entire villages can be displaced by mass rape or the threat of mass rape, which unravels networks that provide social and economic safety nets instrumental to effective recovery.[34]

In situations of conflict and instability around the world—including in Guatemala, Iraq, Libya, and Syria—fear of rape drives families to flee their homes. For example, a 2013 International Rescue Committee study of displaced persons who fled Syria for neighboring Jordan and Lebanon found that a majority identified the danger of rape as a primary reason for leaving cities under siege. Respondents cited numerous instances of women and girls, including young girls, being dragged away and raped at makeshift checkpoints set up by armed groups in regime-controlled areas.[35] Similar concerns have driven displacement in other regions: for instance, threats of abduction spurred the 2014 exodus of two hundred thousand members of the Yazidi community in the Sinjar region of northern Iraq, and Islamic State militants reportedly still hold several thousand Yazidi women in sexual slavery.[36]

Although fear of conflict-related sexual violence drives displacement, those fleeing sexual violence remain vulnerable to attacks once they have left their homes.[37] Women and girls living in refugee camps or as unregistered refugees in informal camps or urban settings face significant risks of sexual violence committed by armed groups, peacekeeping and security forces, and civilians. Attacks frequently occur in overcrowded housing situations or when women and girls leave the relative protection of shelter to use sanitation facilities or collect firewood, water, or other items. In Darfur, for example, rights groups have documented scores of cases of rape of women and girls traveling along rural roads collecting provisions, and almost a third of the victims were raped by multiple perpetrators.[38]

WEAKENED GOVERNANCE

Conflict-related sexual violence also heightens insecurity by signaling a government's inability or unwillingness to protect its citizens, particularly when this crime is perpetrated widely with impunity. The lower the trust in the state, the more difficult it becomes for a government to implement economic, social, or political reforms, thereby limiting the capacity to end a conflict or rebuild after a war has ended.[39] Moreover, youth exposure to acts of violence—including all forms of sexual violence—lessens trust in government institutions, including judicial systems, security forces, and electoral processes.[40] Exposure to such violence reduces cooperative behavior among affected communities and undermines programs and institutions designed to aid victims of conflict, hindering the public provision of goods and services, weakening social networks, and exacerbating economic and political instability.[41]

Declining trust in the government's ability to provide recourse for crimes committed against civilians also feeds grievances against the state, which makes citizens more likely to join or support nonstate armed groups and increases the risk of conflict relapse. In northern Nigeria, for example, although the Boko Haram insurgency is driven by a complex mix of historical, political, economic, and ethnic antagonisms, the perceived inability of the government to effectively neutralize militants and protect villages was exacerbated by slow progress in delivering on its promise to free the nearly three hundred schoolgirls captured from the northern town of Chibok in 2014.[42] A perceptible absence of legal justice for sexual violence survivors leaves citizens vulnerable to exploitation and recruitment by "effective" armed groups.[43]

The effects of conflict-related sexual violence also restrict women's political and civic participation, thereby undermining governance and increasing the likelihood of recurring conflict. An analysis of fifty-eight postconflict states between 1980 and 2003 found that the risk of conflict relapse was near zero when women made up at least 35 percent of the legislature, even when controlling for a host of other factors thought to be associated with relapse. When women were unrepresented in parliaments, however, the risk of relapse increased over time.[44]

HIGHER COSTS

Conflict-related sexual violence imposes direct costs that can plague countries already riven by instability and limited resources. Even after a conflict has ended, the suffering of individual victims of sexual violence persists, including with respect to unwanted pregnancies, sexually transmitted infections, stigmatization, and psychological trauma.[45] Research on the consequences of war cites sexual violence as one reason why women experience more long-term health consequences from conflict than men.[46] Immediate service provision and long-term care for survivors—such as HIV treatment, maternal and child care, and legal redress—exact a financial toll. In addition, violence during wartime is thought to normalize gender-based violence in peacetime, exacerbating the costs of this practice after armed conflict has ceased.[47]

Conflict-related sexual violence also increases the indirect costs of war. Victims of sexual violence can experience long-term physical and psychological consequences, resulting in reduced economic productivity and lost income. In the DRC, for example, agricultural output has decreased partly because women are afraid to return to working in the fields.[48] Stigma also remains a potent force that excludes women from the economic sphere and can result in a loss of marriage prospects, leading to a lifetime of poverty.[49] The economic ramifications of conflict-related sexual violence can compound across generations, because children born of rape frequently experience discrimination and exclusion from services; children born to girls captured by Boko Haram, for example, are stigmatized as having "bad blood" and are significantly more likely to be abused and uneducated.[50]

LOWER PROSPECTS FOR RECONCILIATION

Conflict-related sexual violence, particularly in ethnically or politically driven civil conflict, complicates efforts to bring warring parties to the negotiating table. Sexual violence can unravel kinship ties that hold communities together, thereby undermining reconciliation. In the 1994 Rwandan genocide, for example, thousands of Tutsi women were raped by their Hutu neighbors. This situation presented unique challenges when violence subsided and perpetrators returned to their homes.[51] In many cases, women raped by opposing parties endured a stigma of guilt by association with their perpetrators, and children conceived through acts of rape were considered children of the enemy.[52] As documented in many contexts, sexual violence committed by a perceived enemy can lead to lethal retaliation against the perpetrator or members of his or her identity group, which can foster tensions in a community long after a conflict has subsided; in other cases, sexual violence can lead to so-called honor crimes committed against victims, which can further destabilize communities.[53]

DIMINISHED INTERNATIONAL COOPERATION

Sexual violence committed by peacekeepers and security forces undermines U.S. interests in preserving international institutions that shoulder much of the burden of promoting stability around the world. For example, the epidemic of sexual violence in UN peacekeeping missions badly damages public perceptions of the United Nations within the United States as well as in host countries, thereby weakening the standing and efficacy of multilateral peacekeeping operations critical to U.S. security. The rampant sexual abuse committed by peacekeepers in Haiti, for example, significantly undermined perceptions of the United Nations; indeed, before the Haiti mission's mandate ended in 2017, nearly three-quarters of Haitian media coverage of the peacekeeping mission was negative, and a majority of Haitians disapproved of the mission.[54] In the United States, opponents of multilateralism often cite abuse by UN peacekeepers as a reason to reduce U.S. investment in international institutions across the board, notwithstanding the many ways in which these institutions advance U.S. interests.

Conflict-related sexual violence is also an affront to U.S. values and its commitment to protecting human dignity and human rights. Failure to hold perpetrators of these crimes accountable undermines U.S. standing on other human rights issues, diminishing U.S. influence in current and future security efforts.

Policy Considerations for the United States

In recent years, evidence of the relationship between widespread sexual violence and insecurity has grown, and the United States has begun to pay closer attention to the imperative to prevent and respond to all forms of sexual violence in conflict. Yet more can and should be done.

CURRENT U.S. POLICY

Over the past two decades, the United States has taken steps to elevate the issue of conflict-related sexual violence on the security agenda. A series of UN Security Council resolutions introduced by the United States under the George W. Bush and Barack Obama administrations condemned the use of rape as a tool of war, established a special representative to the UN secretary-general on sexual violence in armed conflict, and created a reporting mechanism to increase accountability (see appendix 2). In recent years, the United States also has collaborated with allies to bring greater international attention to this issue, including through the 2013 Declaration of Commitment to End Sexual Violence in Conflict (signed by 151 countries), the 2014 Global Summit to End Sexual Violence in Conflict (cohosted by the United Kingdom and UN High Commissioner for Refugees Special Envoy Angelina Jolie), and the 2016 UK defense peacekeeping ministerial.[55]

U.S. leadership on conflict-related sexual violence on the world stage has been paired with increased focus on this issue through a new U.S. policy framework on women and security.[56] The *U.S. National Action Plan on Women, Peace, and Security*, last updated in 2016, outlines a strategy to counter conflict-related sexual violence and promote women's participation in peace processes.[57] The Departments of Defense, State, Justice, Treasury, and Homeland Security; the U.S. Mission to the United Nations; the U.S. Agency for International Development

(USAID); the Centers for Disease Control and Prevention; and the Office of the U.S. Trade Representative have all made specific commitments to the plan. Additional commitments were outlined in the *United States Strategy to Prevent and Respond to Gender-Based Violence Globally.*[58] As of August 2017, more than sixty countries have enacted similar national action plans with commitments to counter conflict-related sexual violence, along with regional and multilateral bodies from the African Union to NATO to the Group of Seven (G7).[59]

However, despite the adoption of these plans, the U.S. government has taken only modest steps toward their implementation. Its failure to prioritize the directives under the *U.S. National Action Plan* led a bipartisan coalition in the U.S. Congress to introduce legislation to bolster its implementation, which passed the House of Representatives and the Senate in 2017.

Additionally, the security sector has not taken significant steps to address conflict-related sexual violence. Most efforts have remained detached from broader security-sector initiatives—including the 2013 U.S. security-sector assistance policy and the 2014 U.S. security governance initiative—and investment by the United States in this area has been limited to small grants or stand-alone programs. The United States also has not leveraged its leadership position to encourage other governments to make security-sector commitments on this issue.

RECOMMENDATIONS FOR THE UNITED STATES

The practice of conflict-related sexual violence jeopardizes U.S. interests in stability. Therefore, the U.S. government should prioritize cost-effective interventions to address this security threat. This focus aligns with the Trump administration's robust commitment to advancing U.S. security interests and reforming UN peacekeeping efforts.

Some critics may suggest that expending time and resources to address conflict-related sexual violence constitutes an unnecessary deviation from core U.S. foreign policy and national security priorities at a time of significant security challenges at home and abroad, restricted budgets, and economic uncertainty. However, preventing conflict-related sexual violence will advance core U.S. security interests, given evidence that this practice imperils command and control, increases displacement, weakens governance, and inhibits reconciliation.

Other policymakers may recognize that sexual violence undermines stability, but nevertheless refute the idea that policy reform can garner better results, under the erroneous theory that sexual violence cannot be prevented or adequately redressed. Although it is true that sexual violence is used as a tactic of war and terror, it is not endemic to all conflict, and examples of best practices around the world—from community-based police reforms initiated in Nicaragua in the 1990s to innovative prosecutorial approaches recently instituted in the DRC—demonstrate that progress can be made with relatively modest expenditures (see appendix 3).

To strengthen U.S. efforts to promote stability, the White House—together with USAID and the Departments of Defense, State, Justice, and Treasury, among other agencies—should increase efforts to counter conflict-related sexual violence *before* conflict (by requiring training on conflict-related sexual violence in U.S. security cooperation efforts), *during* conflict (by improving the performance of peacekeeping forces and increasing the proportion of peacekeepers who are women), and *after* conflict (by using financial incentives and diplomatic strategies to increase accountability). Achieving these steps would be facilitated by a full-time senior-ranking coordinating position at the Department of Defense to coordinate, together with the State Department, the security-sector efforts outlined below to prevent conflict-related sexual violence, protect civilians, and promote accountability. The United States also should lead by example here at home by taking meaningful steps to address sexual violence in the U.S. military.

PREVENTION

The 2017 National Defense Authorization Act security cooperation reforms require, for the first time, that security cooperation efforts be accompanied by training on human rights and the law of armed conflict. The Trump administration should build on these reforms by requiring the Defense and State Departments to include—in all U.S. security cooperation efforts—a new scenario-based training protocol to prevent conflict-related sexual violence. The protocol would be drawn from successful training methodologies.[60] U.S. officials also should condition participation in security cooperation programs on the adoption of accountability systems that prohibit the retention or promotion of accused perpetrators and maintain rigorous standards of conduct on sexual violence within national military protocols.

In light of evidence that inclusion of women in security-sector efforts strengthens security operations, the United States should require all countries participating in U.S.-provided security and justice programs—from the International Military Education and Training program to courses offered at the Department of Defense's regional centers—to send delegations that are at least 30 percent female.[61] In addition, to increase the recruitment, retention, and advancement of women, U.S. security cooperation efforts should support quotas of at least 30 percent, accelerated promotion plans, prohibitions on sex discrimination, and technical training for women. To address the root causes of sexual violence, the U.S. government should also launch an annual $5 million small-grants fund to support civil society efforts to address harmful norms and bolster the resistance capacity of women and communities to counter violence and promote postconflict recovery.

PROTECTION

The United States should lead an effort to better prepare peacekeepers to protect civilians from sexual violence. To that end, the United States should support making mandatory a UN protocol for pre-deployment peacekeeper training on protecting civilians from sexual violence, and should, through the Security Council, require UN missions to regularly rehearse contingency plans that address protection of civilians. In addition, the United States should work with partners at the United Nations to bolster incentive payments for troop- and police-contributing countries that demonstrate strong performance on civilian protection.

In addition, the United States should prioritize efforts to reduce the incidence of sexual violence by peacekeepers, which is not only a human rights violation but also a security issue that undermines the credibility of peacekeeping operations. Given evidence that the participation of women in peacekeeping units lowers the risk of sexual violence and improves the reporting of cases, Washington should take steps to support the UN goal of doubling the number of female peacekeepers by 2020.[62] In the run-up to the 2017 UN Peacekeeping Defense Ministerial in Vancouver, the United States should work with the Canadians and other partners to take the following steps: First, to address the lack of women in the peacekeeping pipeline, the U.S. government should partner with the top five police- and troop-contributing countries to launch new initiatives to recruit and retain women in their national forces. Second, to better prepare female officers for deployment, the U.S. government should require that women represent at least 30 percent of local participants in U.S.-led military and police peacekeeper training programs around the world. Current efforts in this direction are already showing success: from August 2011 to August 2016, partners of the U.S. Global Peace Operations Initiative (GPOI) increased their deployment of female military peacekeepers by 62 percent, versus a 24 percent increase among non-GPOI partners.[63] The U.S. government also should participate in and fund UN peacekeeping training for female military officers, which provides professional advancement and networking opportunities. Third, the U.S. government should support efforts to provide financial incentives to police- and troop-contributing countries to increase the number of women deployed. One approach suggests providing a 10 percent premium to countries based on the percentage of women in the contingent, their rank and function, and the contingent's completion of specialized training on gender issues, which would require voluntary contributions of approximately $67.5 million per year.[64]

The United States also should build on successful UN efforts to obtain commitments by nonstate armed groups to prevent and respond to sexual violence perpetrated by their members. At present, U.S. efforts to obtain such commitments from nonstate armed groups could fall under the prohibited material support category of providing "expert advice or assistance" to groups designated as terrorists by the State Department. The Department of Justice should issue a policy clarifying that efforts to solicit and monitor commitments by nonstate armed groups to ban sexual violence will be exempt from prosecution under the material support statute. In the interim, the secretary of state should use existing authorities to approve permitted outreach.[65]

Furthermore, because little attention is paid to male victims of conflict-related sexual violence, the United States should support programs to counter sexual violence against men and boys in conflict situations, including through diplomatic efforts to ensure that legal prohibitions, remedies, and social services are available regardless of gender or sexual orientation.

ACCOUNTABILITY

To discourage the use of sexual violence in conflict by militaries, police, and armed groups, the U.S. government should first lead a coalition of partners—including Canada, the Netherlands, and the United Kingdom—to impose greater accountability for this crime.[66] For example, partner countries could agree to condition bilateral assistance and weapon transfers to foreign militaries on the security units' human rights record, including with respect to sexual violence. Such a commitment would be modeled on the U.S. Leahy Law (1997) and Section 502B of the Foreign Assistance Act, which prohibits the use of funds for units of foreign security forces that have committed gross violations of human rights.[67] A remediation process would allow governments to reinstate their assistance to security units once specific accountability measures have been met.

Second, the United States should encourage partner countries and the UN Security Council to coordinate with Washington by imposing targeted sanctions, including visa bans, on political and military leaders who order or tolerate rape. The United States also should institute a formal policy against assertion of immunities on behalf of peacekeepers sued in domestic courts.

Third, the United States should lead other countries in an organized name-and-shame campaign to highlight incidence of rape among military, police, peacekeepers, or nonstate armed groups. Such an approach will not reach groups or leaders impervious to international legitimacy, but it has proven to constrain the severity of state-sanctioned genocide and other gross human rights violations.[68] As part of this effort, a U.S.-led coalition should pressure the United Nations to remove force commanders who fail to address sexual exploitation and abuse and prioritize redress for victims of sexual violence by peacekeepers.

Fourth, given evidence that sexual violence is used by terrorist entities as a recruitment tool and a source of funding, the Departments of Treasury and State and USAID should work with allies to undermine terrorist financing and block access to assets raised through the abduction of women and children for trafficking, trading, and sexual exploitation. The United States should encourage governments to classify survivors of sexual violence by terrorist or extremist groups as victims of terrorism, thereby ensuring appropriate support.

Fifth, to improve accountability for conflict-related sexual violence, the United States and its partners should insist that parties to cease-fire and peace agreements designate this crime as a breach and prohibit amnesty for those who commit it. Furthermore, the United States should encourage women's participation in peace processes to increase the likelihood that agreements include measures to prevent and ensure accountability for sexual violence. It also should provide targeted assistance to countries to align national laws on sexual violence with international norms so that countries can reliably hold perpetrators of sexual violence accountable.

Finally, the United States should continue its political and financial support for the UN Office of the Special Representative of the Secretary-General for Sexual Violence in Conflict, which offers technical assistance and programs to improve how countries' security and justice sectors address this crime.

LEADING BY EXAMPLE

Both to strengthen the U.S. military and to lead by example, the Department of Defense should elevate its efforts to prevent and respond to sexual assault within the U.S. armed forces. To accelerate reforms, the defense secretary should require quarterly benchmarks from the Office of the Undersecretary of Defense for Personnel and Readiness and the Sexual Assault Prevention and Response Office and report on progress to the U.S. national security advisor. Further reforms enabling the prosecution of violations outside the chain of command should be considered in the absence of meaningful progress. In addition, the United States should take steps to increase the proportion of women in the U.S. military and across law enforcement by doubling recruitment, promotion, and retention efforts and maintaining rigorous implementation of antidiscrimination laws. Furthermore, the U.S. government should require security contractors to implement formal procedures to prevent and respond to sexual violence and sexual harassment of both men and women, meet a 30 percent goal of female recruitment, and vet all personnel to prevent those with previous charges of rape or domestic violence from being hired and deployed.

Conclusion

Preventing and responding to sexual violence committed against civilians in times of conflict is not just the right thing to do—it is a strategic imperative. Substantial evidence confirms that sexual violence fosters insecurity and undermines postconflict reconciliation and stability. To address this security threat, the Trump administration should reform security cooperation to include prevention of conflict-related sexual violence, increase women's participation in the security and judicial sectors, promote accountability for crimes committed during conflict, and ensure that U.S. diplomats and security professionals recognize that addressing sexual violence is critical to stability.

Appendix 1: Governing Legal Principles

Since the 1990s, the International Criminal Court (ICC), International Criminal Tribunal for the Former Yugoslavia (ICTY), International Criminal Tribunal for Rwanda (ICTR), other international tribunals, and national courts have carried out extensive investigations and prosecutions of wartime sexual violence, resulting in historic indictments of sexual violence as a war crime, crime against humanity, and act of genocide.

DUSKO TADIC CASE (1997)

The trial of Dusko Tadic, a Bosnian Serb paramilitary leader, was the first international war crimes trial involving charges of sexual violence. Tadic was found guilty in 1997 of crimes against humanity, including sexual violence against male prisoners.

JEAN-PAUL AKAYESU CASE (1998)

A mayor from the Taba commune in Rwanda stood trial for fifteen counts of genocide and crimes against humanity. The judgment set a precedent that rape can constitute an act of genocide.

SEPUR ZARCO CASE (2016)

Former officers at the Sepur Zarco military base in Guatemala were convicted of crimes against humanity against indigenous Q'eqchi' women who were subjected to sexual violence, sexual and domestic slavery, and forced disappearance of family members. The case was the first time that a national court anywhere in the world either considered or charged conflict-related sexual violence.

JEAN-PIERRE BEMBA CASE (2016)

The trial of the former rebel group leader and vice president of the Democratic Republic of Congo tested the principle of command responsibility for rape, resulting in the first conviction at the ICC for sexual violence as a weapon of war.

HISSENE HABRE CASE (2016)

The former president of Chad was convicted of torture, war crimes, and crimes against humanity, including having raped a woman himself, by the Extraordinary African Chambers in the Senegalese court system, marking the first time the courts of one country convicted the former ruler of another for human rights crimes.

Appendix 2: UN Security Council Resolutions on Sexual Violence in Conflict

UNSCR 1325 (2000) acknowledged the disproportionate impact of armed conflict on women and girls and called for the consideration of women and girls' needs during and after conflict, as well as for an increase in women's participation in all aspects of peace and security processes.

UNSCR 1820 (2008) condemned sexual violence as a weapon of war and declared rape and other forms of sexual violence as war crimes.

UNSCR 1888 (2009) established a special representative to the UN secretary-general on sexual violence in armed conflict and outlined a commitment by the council to include protection from conflict-related sexual violence in peacekeeping mandates.

UNSCR 1960 (2010) created a surveillance mechanism and called for an annual list of all governments and nonstate armed groups suspected of committing conflict-related sexual violence, facilitating a name-and-shame campaign and sanctions.

UNSCR 2106 (2013) emphasized the responsibility of countries to fight impunity by prosecuting those responsible for conflict-related sexual violence and underscored the link between conflict-related sexual violence and broader efforts to reform the security and justice sectors.

UNSCR 2242 (2015) called on the United Nations to double the number of women in peacekeeping operations over the next five years.

UNSCR 2272 (2016) called on the UN secretary-general to replace military or police units when a contributing country fails to hold perpetrators of sexual exploitation and abuse accountable.

UNSCR 2331 (2016) recognized human trafficking and sexual violence as tactics of terrorism used to incentivize recruitment and support financing through the sale of women, girls, and boys.

Appendix 3: Case Studies

A qualitative evaluation of patterns of sexual violence in conflicts of the past twenty years demonstrates how legal and judicial reforms can effectively address this crime. In Colombia, women's participation in peace negotiations led to the inclusion of redress for sexual violence within the resulting peace agreement. In the Democratic Republic of Congo, a political commitment to military justice has improved accountability for the crime of mass rape. In South Sudan, reforms to peacekeeping training and command structure have enhanced protection against conflict-related sexual violence.

COLOMBIA

Throughout Colombia's fifty-year civil conflict, sexual violence was perpetrated in what the country's constitutional court called a "habitual, extensive, systematic, and invisible practice."[69] During the peace process, negotiators on both sides established the world's first gender subcommission, and prominent women's organizations, included at the table, elevated the issue of conflict-related sexual violence on the negotiating agenda.[70] Because of these efforts, the final 2016 peace agreement affirmed that acts of sexual violence constituted crimes against humanity and would be ineligible for amnesty, supported measures to address risks of violence, and created truth and justice mechanisms to prevent impunity for conflict-related sexual violence.[71] Officials also took steps to improve women's access to justice and expand the range of punishable sexual offenses in the penal code. Although the vast majority of cases of sexual violence related to Colombia's armed conflict remain unpunished today—as few as 2 percent of the 635 recorded cases of conflict-related sexual violence resulted in convictions as of 2016—the process nonetheless set an international precedent for the inclusion of conflict-related sexual violence in a peace agreement.[72]

DEMOCRATIC REPUBLIC OF CONGO

During more than twenty years of conflict in the DRC, hundreds of thousands of women and girls (in addition to men and boys) have been sexually violated by various rebel groups and the Congolese army and police, mainly in the country's war-ravaged east. A Human Rights Watch report documented a climate of total impunity in the early years of the 2000s, with commanders condoning sexual violence, even for soldiers who committed gang rapes and rapes leading to injury and death.[73]

Although the justice system remains weak, recent efforts to strengthen it have helped in holding perpetrators accountable. Military prosecutions increased after the Congolese government signed a joint communiqué and framework of cooperation with the United Nations: in 2016, one hundred members of the state security forces were convicted for sexual violence crimes.[74] The Congolese government has held several high-ranking military commanders accountable, and the International Criminal Court convicted former Vice President Jean-Pierre Bemba for crimes against humanity and war crimes related to sexual violence.

Nonetheless, accountability remains wanting for sexual violence committed by members of nonstate armed groups, who were responsible for 68 percent of verified incidents in 2016.[75] Arrests and verdicts have been rendered in several cases—for example, forty militia members involved in the rape of at least fifty children in Kavumu were arrested in 2016 by the national police with assistance from the UN Team of Experts on the Rule of Law/Sexual Violence in Conflict—but the majority of perpetrators of mass sexual violence in Walikale, Bushani, and Kalambahiro have not been held accountable, and reparation payments to victims awarded by Congolese courts remain unpaid.[76]

In recent years, Congolese President Joseph Kabila appointed a presidential advisor on sexual violence and child recruitment, tasked with combating impunity, strengthening the civilian and military justice systems, and improving services for rape victims. In addition, nearly two hundred military field commanders signed commitments to prevent and address sexual violence among their ranks, and three new special police units were formed to respond to sexual violence in the Rutshuru, Goma, and Bukavu jurisdictions.[77] The U.S. government and its partners supported the creation of mobile courts to try rape cases across the country, bringing traveling judges, prosecutors, and defense counsel to remote areas to resolve disputes and dispense justice.[78] Collectively, such measures have made modest but measurable improvements, increasing accountability in a country previously known as the rape capital of the world. However, much more work remains to bring stability and justice to survivors of conflict-related sexual violence in the DRC.

SOUTH SUDAN

Under a current UN Security Council mandate, twelve thousand peace-keepers in South Sudan are authorized to use force when needed to pro-tect civilians from imminent harm, and the South Sudanese UN mission hosts nearly two hundred thousand displaced people in several protec-tion of civilians (PoC) sites.[79] However, a recent UN survey found that 70 percent of women in the PoC sites had been raped—primarily by soldiers or police—since the start of the conflict.[80] Peacekeeping forces also did little to help during an attack by South Sudanese government troops in July 2016, when more than two hundred women—including expatriate aid workers—were sexually assaulted and even gang-raped.[81] The United Nations concluded in a subsequent report that peacekeep-ers retreated or improperly waited for written authorization of force, and peacekeeping command ignored cables requesting backup.[82] Then UN Secretary-General Ban Ki-moon responded by firing the com-mander of the UN peacekeeping forces in South Sudan and calling for increased accountability.[83]

Human Rights Watch and other watchdog groups have repeatedly urged the African Union to establish a hybrid court to try the most seri-ous crimes committed during the South Sudan conflict, and many UN officials have called for better training, clearer chains of command, and better emergency lines of communication to improve UN response to sexual violence. Commanding Officer Colonel Bat-erdene Batkhuu and others cite the actions of Mongolian peacekeeping teams as a best prac-tice to be replicated throughout the mission. Those peacekeepers took strong action to secure protectees, including by rescuing approximately fifty internally displaced people from attempted abduction, preventing the harassment of women and children near a duty station in Bentiu, and robustly defending a PoC site from an attempted breach of the perimeter.[84] Reports suggest that the forty-one female members of the Mongolian peacekeeping team made critical contributions by improv-ing communication with the local community under protection.[85]

Endnotes

1. Conflict-related sexual violence as defined by the United Nations can take the form of rape, sexual slavery, forced prostitution, forced pregnancy, forced abortion, enforced sterilization, forced marriage, and any other form of sexual violence of comparable gravity perpetrated against women, men, girls, or boys that is linked to a conflict.
2. See, for example, the cases against Agnes Ntamabyariro and Pauline Nyiramasuhuko for crimes against humanity in Rwanda, including ordering, aiding, and abetting rape. See Kirsten Johnson, Jennifer Scott, Bigy Rughita, Michael Kisielewski, Jana Asher, Ricardo Ong, and Lynn Lawry, "Association of Sexual Violence and Human Rights Violations with Physical and Mental Health in Territories of the Eastern Democratic Republic of the Congo," *Journal of the American Medical Association* 304, no. 5, 2010, pp. 553–62; Lisa Sharlach, "Gender and Genocide in Rwanda: Women as Agents and Objects of Genocide," *Journal of Genocide Research* 1, no. 3, 1999; Peter Landesman, "A Woman's Work," *New York Times Magazine*, September 15, 2002, http://www.nytimes.com/2002/09/15/magazine/a-woman-s-work.html?mcubz=1.
3. United Nations (UN), "Report of the Secretary-General on Conflict-Related Sexual Violence," S/2017/249, April 15, 2017, http://www.un.org/en/events/elimination-of-sexual-violence-in-conflict/pdf/1494280398.pdf.
4. Dara Kay Cohen and Ragnhild Nordås, "Do States Delegate Shameful Violence to Militias? Patterns of Sexual Violence in Recent Armed Conflicts," *Journal of Conflict Resolution* 59, no. 5, 2015, pp. 877–98.
5. Dara Kay Cohen, "Explaining Rape During Civil War: Cross-National Evidence (1980–2009)," August 2013, http://www.belfercenter.org/publication/explaining-rape-during-civil-war-cross-national-evidence-1980-2009; Ragnhild Nordås, "Sexual Violence in African Conflicts," CSCW Policy Brief No. 1, Peace Research Institute Oslo, 2011, https://www.prio.org/utility/DownloadFile.ashx?id=204&type=publicationfile.
6. Dara Kay Cohen, Amelia Hoover Green, and Elisabeth Jean Wood, "Wartime Sexual Violence," Special Report no. 323, United States Institute of Peace, February 2013, https://www.usip.org/sites/default/files/resources/SR323.pdf.
7. Dara Kay Cohen, *Rape During Civil War* (Ithaca, NY: Cornell University Press, 2016).
8. UN, "Conflict-Related Sexual Violence."
9. UN Regional Information Centre for Western Europe, "Sexual Violence: The Silent Weapon of War," June 2017, https://unric.org/en/latest-un-buzz/30599-sexual-violence-the-silent-weapon-of-war.
10. UN, "Report of the Secretary-General on Conflict-Related Sexual Violence."
11. Ana Swanson, "How the Islamic State Makes Its Money," *Washington Post*, November 2015, https://www.washingtonpost.com/news/wonk/wp/2015/11/18/how-isis-makes-its-money/.

12. UN, "Conflict-Related Sexual Violence"; UN, "Sexual Violence: A Tool of War," Background Note, April 1998, http://www.un.org/en/preventgenocide/rwanda/pdf /Backgrounder%20Sexual%20Violence%202013.pdf; Sergey Marochkin and Galina Nelaeva, "Rape and Sexual Violence as Torture and Genocide in the Decisions of International Tribunals," *Human Rights Review* 15, no. 4, December 2014, https://link .springer.com/article/10.1007/s12142-014-0322-6.

13. Cohen, *Rape During Civil War*; Michele Leiby, "Wartime Sexual Violence in Guatemala and Peru," *International Studies Quarterly*, 2009, http://www.micheleleiby.com /downloads/isq_wartime_sexual_violence.pdf; Human Rights Watch (HRW), "'No One Is Safe': Abuses of Women in Iraq's Criminal Justice System," February 6, 2014, https://www.hrw.org/report/2014/02/06/no-one-safe/abuse-women-iraqs-criminal -justice-system; Kevin Redmon, "The New Abu Ghraib," *Atlantic*, May 2010, https://www.theatlantic.com/international/archive/2010/05/the-new-abu-ghraib /39841/; Marie Forestier, "Rape as a Tactic of the Assad Regime," *Centre for Women, Peace + Security* (blog), March 2017, http://blogs.lse.ac.uk/wps/2017/02/01/you-want -freedom-this-is-your-freedom-rape-as-a-tactic-of-the-assad-regime-marie-forestier -32016/; Jennifer Lynn Green, "Collective Rape: A Cross-National Study of the Incidence and Perpetrators of Mass Political Sexual Violence, 1980–2003" (Ph.D. diss., Ohio State University, 2006).

14. Cohen, Green, and Wood, "Wartime Sexual Violence"; Dara Kay Cohen and Ragnhild Nordas, "Sexual Violence in African Conflicts, 1989–2009," CSCW Policy Brief no. 2, Peace Research Institute Oslo, 2012, http://file.prio.no/publication_files/cscw /Nordas-Cohen-Sexual-Violence-in-African-Conflicts-1989-2009-CSCW-Policy -Brief-02-2012.pdf.

15. UN, "Conflict-Related Sexual Violence"; Sara Meger, *Rape Loot Pillage: The Political Economy of Sexual Violence in Armed Conflict* (Oxford: Oxford University Press, 2016), http://www.oxfordscholarship.com/view/10.1093/acprof:oso/9780190277666.001 .0001/acprof-9780190277666.

16. Cohen, Green, and Wood, "Wartime Sexual Violence"; Cohen and Nordås, "Sexual Violence in African Conflicts."

17. Cohen, Green, and Wood, "Wartime Sexual Violence."

18. The term *sexual exploitation and abuse* describes forms of sexual violence that involve abuse, by force or under coercive conditions, of a position of vulnerability, differential power, or trust for sexual purposes. The term applies to sexual violence committed by any staff of the United Nations against members of a vulnerable population and is prohibited under Provision ST/SGB/2003/13 (UN, "Glossary on Sexual Exploitation and Abuse," October 5, 2016, http://reliefweb.int/sites/reliefweb.int/files/resources/ un_glossary_on_sea.pdf; Benedetta Faedi Duramy, "From Violence Against Women to Women's Violence in Haiti," *Columbia Journal of Gender and Law* 19, no. 4, 2010, p.1029, http://digitalcommons.law.ggu.edu/cgi/viewcontent.cgi?article=1571&context =pubs; Associated Press, "UN Child Sex Ring Left Victims but No Arrests," April 12, 2017, https://www.apnews.com/e6ebc331460345c5abd4f57d77f535c1/AP-Exclusive :-UN-child-sex-ring-left-victims-but-no-arrests).

19. UN News Centre, "Killings, Rapes in South Sudan Continued 'Unabated' After July 2016 Violence, UN Reports," January 16, 2017, http://www.un.org/apps/news/story .asp?NewsID=55975#.WVFUVvvyu70; UN Office of the High Commissioner for Human Rights (OHCHR), "South Sudan: UN Report Contains 'Searing' Account of Killings, Rapes and Destruction," March 11, 2016, http://www.ohchr.org/EN /NewsEvents/Pages/DisplayNews.aspx?NewsID=17207&LangID=E.

20. Zainab Salbi, "ISIS Recruits Young Syrians with the Promise of Wives from the 'Women's Market,'" *New York Times*, May 2016, https://nytlive.nytimes.com /womenintheworld/2016/05/24/isis-recruits-young-syrians-with-the-promise-of -wives-from-the-womens-market/; Mia Bloom, "How ISIS Is Using Marriage as a Trap," *The WorldPost*, 2016, http://www.huffingtonpost.com/mia-bloom/isis-marriage -trap_b_6773576.html; David Denby, "The Perfect Children of ISIS," *New Yorker*, November 2015, http://www.newyorker.com/culture/cultural-comment/the-perfect -children-of-isis-lessons-from-dabiq.

21. Institute for Strategic Dialogue, "Till Martyrdom Do Us Part: Gender and the ISIS Phenomenon," 2015, http://www.strategicdialogue.org/wp-content/uploads/2016/02 /Till_Martyrdom_Do_Us_Part_Gender_and_the_ISIS_Phenomenon.pdf.

22. International Crisis Group (ICG), "Nigeria: Women and the Boko Haram Insurgency," Report no. 242, December 2016, https://www.crisisgroup.org/africa/west-africa /nigeria/nigeria-women-and-boko-haram-insurgency.

23. Cohen, *Rape During Civil War*.

24. Ibid.

25. International Committee of the Red Cross, "Geneva Convention Relative to the Pro-tection of Civilian Persons in Time of War (Fourth Geneva Convention)," August 1949, https://treaties.un.org/doc/publication/unts/volume%2078/volume-78-i-1021 -english.pdf.

26. Catherine A. Mackinnon, "Genocide's Sexuality," *Nomos* 46, 2005, pp. 209–33; Editorial Board, "When Rape Becomes Genocide," *New York Times*, September 5, 1998, http://www.nytimes.com/1998/09/05/opinion/when-rape-becomes-genocide .html; Lauren Wolfe, "Reckoning With a Genocide in Guatemala," *Women Under Siege* (blog), February 2012, http://www.womensmediacenter.com/women-under-siege /reckoning-with-a-genocide-in-guatemala.

27. Binaifer Nowrojee, "Shattered Lives" (New York: HRW, September 1996), https://www .hrw.org/sites/default/files/reports/1996_Rwanda_%20Shattered%20Lives.pdf.

28. HRW, "Burma: Security Forces Raped Rohingya Women, Girls," February 6, 2017, https://www.hrw.org/news/2017/02/06/burma-security-forces-raped-rohingya -women-girls.

29. Stop Rape Now, "Congolese Women Again Bear the Brunt of Undisciplined Secu-rity Forces," Statement by the Special Representative of the Secretary-General on Sexual Violence in Conflict Margot Wallström, June 23, 2011, http://www.un.org /sexualviolenceinconflict/wp-content/uploads/2012/07/SRSG-Statement-on -Congolese-Women-23-June-2011.pdf.

30. UN, "Matrix: Early Warning Indicators of Conflict-Related Sexual Vio-lence," 2011, http://peacemaker.un.org/sites/peacemaker.un.org/files /MatrixEarlyWarningIndicatorsCSV_UNAction2011.pdf; United Nations, "Conflict-Related Sexual Violence."

31. North Atlantic Treaty Organization, "Taking Action on Conflict-Related Sexual and Gender-Based Violence," October 19, 2016, http://www.nato.int/cps/en/natohq/news _136168.htm.

32. See "Women, Peace, and Inclusive Security," special issue, *PRISM* 6, no. 1, March 2016, pp. 2–210; Kim Lonsway et al., "Gender Sensitive Police Reform in Post Conflict So-cieties," UN Development Fund for Women and UN Development Program, October 2007, http://unwomen.org/~/media/Headquarters/ Media/Publications/UNIFEM /GenderSensitivePoliceReformPolicyBrief2007eng. pdf; Tara Denham, "Police Reform and Gender," Geneva Center for the Democratic Control of Armed Forces (DCAF), 2008.

33. World Bank, "Forced Displacement and Development," March 25, 2016, http://siteresources.worldbank.org/DEVCOMMINT/Documentation/23713856/DC2016-0002-FDD.pdf.

34. Nicola Jones, Janice Cooper, Elizabeth Presler-Marshall, and David Walker, "The Fall-out of Rape as a Weapon of War," Overseas Development Institute, 2012, http://cdn.basw.co.uk/upload/basw_100421-5.pdf.

35. International Rescue Committee, "Syria Displacement Crisis Worsens as Protracted Humanitarian Emergency Looms," Press Release, January 14, 2013, https://www.rescue.org/press-release/syria-displacement-crisis-worsens-protracted-humanitarian-emergency-looms.

36. HRW, "UN Panel Reports on ISIS Crimes on Yezidis," June 21, 2016, https://www.hrw.org/news/2016/06/21/un-panel-reports-isis-crimes-yezidis.

37. "Guiding Principles on Internal Displacement," Annex to U.N. Doc. E/CN.4/1998/53/Add.2, "Further Promotion and Encouragement of Human Rights and Fundamental Freedoms, Including the Question of the Programme and Methods of Work of the Commission on Human Rights, Mass Exoduses and Displaced Persons: Report of the Representative of the Secretary-General, Mr. Francis M. Deng, Submitted Pursuant to Commission Resolution 1997/39," February 11, 1998; HRW, "No Protection: Rape and Sexual Violence Following Displacement," April 12, 2005, https://www.hrw.org/legacy/backgrounder/africa/darfur0505/3.htm; Donald Steinberg, "Preventing and Responding to Sexual Violence Against Women Displaced by Conflict," ICG, July 2010, https://www.crisisgroup.org/global/preventing-and-responding-sexual-violence-against-women-displaced-conflict.

38. HRW, "No Protection."

39. UN Department of Economic and Social Affairs and UNDP, "The Challenges of Restoring Governance in Crisis and Postconflict Countries," 2007, https://publicadministration.un.org/publications/content/PDFs/E-Library%20Archives/2007%20The%20Challenges%20of%20Restoring%20Governance%20in%20Crisis%20and%20Postconflict%20Countries.pdf; Alexander De Juan and Jan Pierskalla, "Civil War Violence and Political Trust: Microlevel Evidence From Nepal," *Conflict Management and Peace Science* 33, no. 1, 2016, pp. 67–88, http://journals.sagepub.com/doi/abs/10.1177/0738894214544612.

40. Michelle L. Cullen and Nat J. Colletta, "Violent Conflict and the Transformation of Social Capital: Lessons from Cambodia, Rwanda, Guatemala, and Somalia," World Bank, 2000, http://documents.worldbank.org/curated/en/799651468760532921/Violent-conflict-and-the-transformation-of-social-capital-lessons-from-Cambodia-Rwanda-Guatemala-and-Somalia; Robert Putnam and Lewis Feldstein, *Better Together: Restoring the American Community* (New York: Simon & Schuster, 2003).

41. Cullen and Colletta, "Violent Conflict and the Transformation of Social Capital"; Putnam and Feldstein, *Better Together.*

42. Patricio Asfura-Heim and Julia McQuaid, "Diagnosing the Boko Haram Conflict: Grievances, Motivations, and Institutional Resilience in Northeast Nigeria," CNA Analysis & Solutions, January 2015, https://www.cna.org/cna_files/pdf/DOP-2014-U-009272-Final.pdf.

43. UN, "Conflict-Related Sexual Violence."

44. Jacqueline H. R. DeMeritt et al., "Female Participation and Civil War Relapse," *Civil Wars* 16, no. 3, 2014, p. 362; Marie O'Reilly, "Why Women? Inclusive Security and Peaceful Societies," *Inclusive Security*, October 2015, https://www.inclusivesecurity.org/publication/why-women-inclusive-security-and-peaceful-societies/.

45. James Fearon and Anke Hoeffler, "Benefits and Costs of the Conflict and Violence Targets for the Post-2015 Development Agenda," Copenhagen Consensus Center, 2015, http://www.copenhagenconsensus.com/sites/default/files/conflict_assessment_-_hoeffler_and_fearon_0.pdf.

46. Eric Neumayer and Thomas Plumper, "The Unequal Burden of War: The Effect of Armed Conflict on the Gender Gap in Life Expectancy," *International Organization* 60, no. 3, Summer 2006, pp. 723–54.

47. The costs of violence against women are significant; one study estimates that domestic violence costs $8 trillion globally each year, representing losses of more than 11 percent of global GDP (see Fearon and Hoeffler, "Benefits and Costs"; Carolin Williams, "How to Calculate the Cost to Business of Gender-Based Violence in Papua New Guinea," ODI, April, 2014, http://www.refworld.org/pdfid/53d0c08d4.pdf; David Walker and Nata Duvvury, "Costing the Impacts of Gender-Based Violence [GBV] to Business: A Practical Tool," ODI, February 2016, https://www.odi.org/publications/10298-gbv-papua-new-guinea).

48. Jocelyn Kelly, Michael VanRooyen, Justin Kabanga, Beth Maclin, and Colleen Mullen, "Hope for the Future Again: Tracing the Effects of Sexual Violence and Conflict on Families and Communities in Eastern DRC," Harvard Humanitarian Initiative, 2011, http://hhi.harvard.edu/sites/default/files/publications/hope-for-the-future-again.pdf.

49. Charlotte Lindsey-Curtet, Florence Tercier Holst-Roness, and Letitia Anderson, "Addressing the Needs of Women Affected by Armed Conflict: An ICRC Guidance Document," International Committee of the Red Cross (ICRC), March 2004, https://www.icrc.org/eng/assets/files/other/icrc_002_0840_women_guidance.pdf; Elisabeth Jean Wood, "Conflict-Related Sexual Violence and the Policy Implications of Recent Research," ICRC, 2015.

50. Stephanie Sinclair, "Child, Bride, Mother: Nigeria," *New York Times*, January 27, 2017, https://www.nytimes.com/interactive/2017/01/27/sunday-review/29Exposures-child-bride-interactive.html; Kimberly Theidon, "Hidden in Plain Sight: Children Born of Wartime Sexual Violence," *openSecurity*, September 2015, https://www.opendemocracy.net/opensecurity/kimberly-theidon/hidden-in-plain-sight-children-born-of-wartime-sexual-violence.

51. Article 1 of the Statute of the International Tribunal for Rwanda provides as follows: "The International Tribunal for Rwanda shall have the power to prosecute persons responsible for serious violation of international humanitarian law committed in the territory of Rwanda and Rwandan citizens responsible for such violations committed in the territory of neighboring States, between 1 January 1994 and 31 December 1994." UN Security Council Resolution 955 (1994) Establishing the International Tribunal for Rwanda, Annex.

52. Shada Rouhani, Jennifer Scott, Ashley Greiner, Katherine Albutt, Michele R. Hacker, Philipp Kuwert, Michael VanRooyen, and Susan Bartels, "Stigma and Parenting Children Conceived From Sexual Violence," *Journal of Pediatrics* 136, no. 5, November 2015, https://www.ncbi.nlm.nih.gov/pmc/articles/PMC4890150/; Elisa van Ee amd Rolf J. Kleber, "Growing Up Under a Shadow: Key Issues in Research on and Treatment of Children Born of Rape," *Child Abuse Review* 22, no. 6, 2013, pp. 386–97; R. Charli Carpenter, *Born of War: Protecting Children of Sexual Violence Survivors in Conflict Zones* (Bloomfield, CT: Kumarian Press, 2007); R. Charli Carpenter, "War's Impact on Children Born of Rape and Sexual Exploitation: Physical, Economic, and Psychosocial Dimensions," Coalition to Stop the Use of Child Soldiers, 2005, www.childsoldiersglobalreport.org/content/facts-and-figures-child-soldiers.

53. UN, "Conflict-Related Sexual Violence."

54. Michel Forst, "Technical Assistance and Capacity-Building: Report of the Independent Expert on the Situation of Human Rights in Haiti," UN Human Rights Council, March 2009, http://www2.ohchr.org/english/bodies/hrcouncil/docs/11session/A.HRC.11.5.pdf.

55. United Kingdom Foreign & Commonwealth Office, "A Declaration of Commitment to End Sexual Violence in Conflict," September 2013, https://www.gov.uk/government/publications/a-declaration-of-commitment-to-end-sexual-violence-in-conflict; John Kerry and William Hague, "Preventing Sexual Violence Is a National Security Imperative," *Huffington Post*, http://www.huffingtonpost.com/johnkerry/preventing-sexual-violenc_b_4856070.html.

56. Kerry F. Crawford, *Wartime Sexual Violence* (Washington, DC: Georgetown University Press, 2017), http://press.georgetown.edu/book/georgetown/wartime-sexual-violence.

57. White House, *The United States Action Plan on Women, Peace, and Security*, June 2016, https://www.usaid.gov/sites/default/files/documents/1868/National%20Action%20Plan%20on%20Women%2C%20Peace%2C%20and%20Security.pdf.

58. U.S. Department of State, *Strategy to Prevent and Respond to Gender-Based Violence Globally*, June 2016, https://www.state.gov/documents/organization/258703.pdf.

59. G7 Foreign Ministers, "Joint Communiqué: G7 Foreign Ministers Meeting," April 2017, http://www.mofa.go.jp/files/000246365.pdf; "National Action Plans for the Implementation of UNSCR 1325 on Women, Peace, and Security," August 2017, http://www.peacewomen.org/member-states.

60. Susanne Axmacher, "Review of Scenario-Based Trainings for Military Peacekeepers on Prevention and Response to Conflict-Related Sexual Violence," Stop Rape Now, December 2013, http://stoprapenow.org/uploads/advocacyresources/1394227122.pdf.

61. Empirical analyses strongly suggest that women's participation strengthens security operations, including by improving dispute resolution, enhancing community perception of security force integrity, and increasing access to locations and populations that are off limits to men in traditional societies, thereby strengthening intelligence capabilities. See Francesco Bertolazzi, "Women with a Blue Helmet," UN International Research and Training Institute for the Advancement of Women, 2010, http://www.peacewomen.org/assets/file/Resources/UN/unbalpk_integrationwomengenderunpeacekeeping_instraw_aug_2010.pdf; Sabrina Karim and Kyle Beardsley, "Explaining Sexual Exploitation and Abuse in Peacekeeping Missions: The Role of Female Peacekeepers and Gender Equality in Contributing Countries," *Journal of Peace Research* 53, no. 1, 2016, pp. 100–15, http://journals.sagepub.com/doi/abs/10.1177/0022343315615506; analysis of police representation data from the UN Office on Drugs and Crime and sexual assault reporting calculated from the International Crime Victims Survey, in Laura Turquet et al., *Progress of the World's Women: In Pursuit of Justice* (New York: United Nations Entity for Gender Equality and the Empowerment of Women, 2011); Rosabeth Moss Kanter, *Men and Women of the Corporation* (New York: Basic Books, 1997), pp. 381–95.

62. Louise Olsson and Johan Tejpar, *Operational Effectiveness and UN Resolution 1325 - Practices and Lessons from Afghanistan* (Stockholm: Swedish Defence Research Agency, May 2009), pp. 117, 126–27; Institute for Inclusive Security, "Attention to Gender Increases Security in Operations: Examples from the North Atlantic Treaty Organization (NATO)," April 2012, pp. 7–13, 41; Amalia R. Miller and Carmit Segal, "Do Female Officers Improve Law Enforcement Quality? Effects on Crime Reporting and Domestic Violence Escalation," UBS International Center of Economics in Society at the University of Zurich, August 2014, p. 4; Turquet et al., *Progress of the World's Women*, pp. 59–61.

63. U.S. Department of State, "U.S. Peacekeeping Capacity Building Assistance," Bureau of Political-Military Affairs, January 2017, https://www.state.gov/t/pm/rls/fs/2017 /266854.htm.

64. See UN Security Council Resolution 2242; Center for Global Development, "Using Financial Incentives to Increase the Number of Women in UN Peacekeeping," October 2016, https://www.cgdev.org/publication/using-financial-incentives-increase-number -women-un-peacekeeping; U.S. Department of State, "U.S. Peacekeeping Capacity Building Assistance"; UN Women, "Exploratory Options on Using Financial Incentives to Increase the Percentage of Military Women in UN Peacekeeping Missions," Policy Brief, January 2015, http://wps.unwomen.org/resources/briefs/financial.pdf.

65. See 18 U.S. Code 2339B - Providing Material Support or Resources to Designated Foreign Terrorist Organizations; Claudia Hofmann and Ulrich Schneckener, "NGOs and Nonstate Armed Actors Improving Compliance with International Norms," Special Report no. 284, United States Institute of Peace, July 2011, https://www.usip .org/sites/default/files/sr284.pdf; UN, "Communiqué of the Special Representative of the Secretary-General on Sexual Violence in Conflict, Zainab Hawa Bangura, to Commemorate the National Day for the Dignity of Women Victims of Sexual Violence in the Internal Armed Conflict in Colombia," Press Communiqué, May 26, 2015, http://www.un.org/sexualviolenceinconflict/press-release/communique-of -the-special-representative-of-the-secretary-general-on-sexual-violence-in-conflict -zainab-hawa-bangura-to-commemorate-the-national-day-for-the-dignity-of-women -victims-of-sexual-viole/; UN, "South Sudan: SPLM/SPLA in Opposition Make Commitment to Prevent Conflict-Related Sexual Violence," February 2015, http:// www.un.org/sexualviolenceinconflict/press-release/south-sudan-splmspla-in -opposition-make-commitment-to-prevent-conflict-related-sexual-violence/; Sam Adelsberg, Freya Pitts, and Sirine Shebaya, "The Chilling Effect of the 'Material Support' Law on Humanitarian Aid: Causes, Consequences, and Proposed Reforms," Harvard University, 2013, http://harvardnsj.org/wp-content/uploads/2013/01/Vol -4-Adelsberg-Pitts-Shebaya.pdf.

66. Kate Cronin-Furman, "Managing Expectations: International Criminal Trials and the Prospects for Deterrence of Mass Atrocity," *International Journal of Transitional Justice* 7, no. 3, 2013, pp. 434–54, http://www.katecroninfurman.com/research.html.

67. See Provision A of the Leahy Law (1997): "No assistance shall be furnished under this Act or the Arms Export Control Act to any unit of the security forces of a foreign country if the Secretary of State has credible information that such unit has committed a gross violation of human rights." The State Department interprets such violations to include extrajudicial killing, rape, torture, and forced disappearances.

68. Jacqueline R. DeMeritt, "International Organizations and Government Killing: Does Naming and Shaming Save Lives?" *International Interactions* 38, no. 5, 2012, http:// www.tandfonline.com/doi/abs/10.1080/03050629.2012.726180; Matthew Krain, "Does Naming and Shaming Perpetrators Reduce the Severity of Genocides or Politicides?" *International Studies Quarterly* 56, no. 3, 2012, pp. 574–89.

69. Nina M. Birkeland, Edmund Jennings, and Elizabeth J. Rushing, eds., "Global Overview 2011: People Internally Displaced by Conflict and Violence," IMC/NRC, 2012; Organización Indígena de Colombia, "Mujeres indígenas, víctimas invisibles del conflicto armado en Colombia: La violencia sexual, una estrategia de guerra," May 2012.

70. Virginia M. Bouvier, "Gender and the Role of Women in Colombia's Peace Process" (New York: UN Women, March 2016), https://www.usip.org/publications/2016/11 /gender-and-role-women-colombias-peace-process.

71. Jacqueline O'Neill, "Colombia's Inclusive Peace Deal Is at Risk," Council on Foreign Relations, October 2016, https://www.cfr.org/blog-post/colombias-inclusive-peace-deal-risk.

72. UN, "Press Statement by the Special Representative of the Secretary-General on Sexual Violence in Conflict, Zainab Hawa Bangura," June 24, 2014, http://www.un.org/sexualviolenceinconflict/press-release/press-statement-by-the-special-representative-of-the-secretary-general-on-sexual-violence-in-conflict-zainab-hawa-bangura/; Telesur, "97% of Colombia's Cases of Sexual Violence Remain Unpunished," March 2016, http://www.telesurtv.net/english/news/97-of-Colombias-Cases-of-Sexual-Violence-Remain-Unpunished--20160308-0035.html.

73. Human Rights Watch, "Soldiers Who Rape, Commanders Who Condone: Sexual Violence and Military Reform in the Democratic Republic of Congo," July 2009, https://www.hrw.org/report/2009/07/16/soldiers-who-rape-commanders-who-condone/sexual-violence-and-military-reform.

74. United Nations, "United Nations Team of Experts on Rule of Law/Sexual Violence in Conflict 2016 Annual Report," July 2016.

75. Ibid.

76. Micah Williams and Will Cragin, "Our Experience in Luvungi," *Foreign Policy*, March 2013, http://foreignpolicy.com/2013/03/05/our-experience-in-luvungi/; UN, "U.N. Office of the High Commissioner for Human Rights Released a Final Report of U.N. Fact-Finding Missions," July 2011, http://www.refworld.org/docid/4e1599bc2.html.

77. UN, "United Nations Team of Experts."

78. Open Society Foundations, "Justice in DRC: Mobile Courts Combat Rape and Impunity in Eastern Congo," January 2013, https://www.opensocietyfoundations.org/publications/justice-drc-mobile-courts-combat-rape-and-impunity-eastern-congo.

79. Centers for Civilians in Conflict, "Under Fire: The July 2016 Violence in Juba and UN Response," October 2016, http://civiliansinconflict.org/resources/pub/under-fire-the-july-2016-violence-in-juba-and-un-response.

80. OHCHR, "Statement by Yasmin Sooka, Chair of the Commission on Human Rights in South Sudan at the 26th Special Session of the UN Human Rights Council," December 14, 2016, http://www.ohchr.org/EN/NewsEvents/Pages/DisplayNews.aspx?NewsID=21028&LangID.

81. Merrit Kennedy, "Witnesses: U.N. Peacekeepers Did Nothing as South Sudanese Soldiers Raped Women," NPR, July 27, 2016, http://www.npr.org/sections/thetwo-way/2016/07/27/487625112/report-u-n-peacekeepers-did-nothing-as-south-sudanese-soldiers-raped-women.

82. HRW, "UN Peacekeepers Turn Blind Eye to Rape in South Sudan," 2016, https://www.hrw.org/news/2016/11/03/un-peacekeepers-turn-blind-eye-rape-south-sudan.

83. HRW, "UN: Act on South Sudan Investigations," 2016, https://www.hrw.org/news/2016/06/22/un-act-south-sudan-investigations.

84. UN Mission in South Sudan (UNMISS), "Mongolian Peacekeepers Awarded Medal in South Sudan," May 9, 2017, https://unmiss.unmissions.org/mongolian-peacekeepers-awarded-un-medal-south-sudan.

85. See UNMISS, "UNMISS Mongolian Peacekeepers' Presence Improves Freedom of Movement in Leer County," March 26, 2016, https://unmiss.unmissions.org/unmiss-mongolian-peacekeepers%E2%80%99-presence-improves-freedom-movement-leer-county; UNMISS Media, "The Mongolian Women Peacekeepers," July 28, 2015, https://vimeo.com/134712226.

About the Authors

Jamille Bigio is a senior fellow in the Women and Foreign Policy program at the Council on Foreign Relations. In the Barack Obama administration, Bigio served as director for human rights and gender on the White House National Security Council staff. From 2009 to 2013, Bigio served as senior advisor to U.S. Ambassador-at-Large for Global Women's Issues Melanne Verveer at the Department of State. In addition, Bigio was detailed to the office of the undersecretary of defense for policy and to the U.S. Mission to the African Union. Bigio led the interagency launch of the U.S. National Action Plan on Women, Peace, and Security, an effort for which she was recognized with the U.S. Department of State Superior Honor Award and the U.S. Department of Defense Secretary of Defense Honor Award. Previously, at the United Nations, she worked to strengthen disaster management in Africa and the Middle East. Bigio graduated Phi Beta Kappa from the University of Maryland and received her master's degree from the Harvard Kennedy School.

Rachel Vogelstein is the Douglas Dillon senior fellow and director of the Women and Foreign Policy program at the Council on Foreign Relations and a visiting fellow at Yale Law School's Center for Global Legal Challenges. From 2009 to 2012, Vogelstein was director of policy and senior advisor in the Office of Global Women's Issues within the Office of the Secretary of State at the U.S. Department of State and served as a member of the White House Council on Women and Girls. Following her tenure at the State Department, Vogelstein served as the director of women and girls programs in the Office of Hillary Clinton at the Clinton Foundation, where she oversaw the development of the No Ceilings initiative and provided guidance on domestic and global women's issues. Prior to joining the State Department, Vogelstein served as senior counsel at the National Women's Law Center in Washington,

DC, where she specialized in women's health and reproductive rights. Vogelstein graduated magna cum laude from Columbia University's Barnard College and cum laude from Georgetown University's Law Center, where she was executive editor of the *Georgetown Law Journal*.

Advisory Committee for
Countering Sexual Violence in Conflict

Hamsatu Allamin
*Nigeria Stability and Reconciliation Program /
Federation of Muslim Women Association
in Nigeria*

Patrick Cammaert
*Former Military Advisor to the
Department for Peacekeeping Operations
for the United Nations*

Christine Chinkin
*London School of Economics, Centre
for Women, Peace, and Security*

Dara Kay Cohen
Harvard Kennedy School of Government

Ambassador Ryan Crocker
Texas A&M University

Daniel De Torres
DCAF

Ambassador Paula Dobriansky
Harvard Kennedy School of Government

Nobel Laureate Leymah Gbowee
Gbowee Peace Foundation Africa

Jean-Marie Guéhenno
International Crisis Group

Brigid Inder
*International Criminal Court and Women's
Initiatives for Gender Justice*

Harold Hongju Koh
Yale Law School

Ambassador Princeton Lyman
United States Institute of Peace

Tom Malinowski
*Former U.S. Assistant Secretary of State
for Democracy, Human Rights, and Labor*

Ambassador Stephen Rapp
*Former U.S. Ambassador-at-Large
for Global Criminal Justice*

Paul Stares
Council on Foreign Relations

Anne Witkowsky
*Former U.S. Deputy Assistant Secretary of
Defense for Stability and Humanitarian Affairs*

www.ingramcontent.com/pod-product-compliance
Lightning Source LLC
Chambersburg PA
CBHW071348290326
41933CB00041B/3111